WHERE'S THE MONEY!?

Unleash Your Full Earning Potential

by

Ish Global

ISBN: 978-1-7397553-0-0

UNITED KINGDOM

DEDICATION:

The importance of decision making is a crucial aspect highlighted throughout this book. The person who helped me formulate the foundations of my decision-making ability was my mother, so I would love to dedicate this book to her.

Table of Contents

INTRODUCTION

I'm going to start by telling you something that makes you not want to read the rest of this book. *clears throat* I have only read two books (excluding textbooks) in my entire life.

Are you still there?

If so, let me explain.

I graduated from Loughborough University with a degree in Banking, Finance and Management (BSc). I furthered my business acumen by working for Morgan Stanley, Goldman Sachs and Ernst & Young. Outside of the corporate world, I organise events, have a fashion line (CR8TOR World), and run a social hub. I like to try my hand at things that pique my interest, so I have picked up a range of skills and built a vast network.

I process visual information best. i.e., I prefer to watch interviews and tutorials compared to reading articles and manuals. This probably explains why Upper Echelon UK (one of my ventures) is centred around providing interviews and behind-the-scenes footage to our audience. It is natural for humans to create things they desire because we assume other people will also have these desires.

A few weeks before writing this book, I had my first public event scheduled for Upper Echelon UK, received a financial offer from an investor, and had a holiday booked to Dubai for my birthday. They were all cancelled, put on hold, or rescheduled due to the coronavirus.

I'm going to be completely honest… I was fuming. However, I have a rule; once I have my first sleep after hearing bad news, I move on from it and stop feeling sorry for myself. This always leads to me finding solutions or alternatives after getting out of bed.

"In every crisis, there's an opportunity."

After saying this out loud a few times, it motivated me to use my time to think of a new skill I could develop during the pandemic. I began to highlight areas in my life that I could improve on, and the number of books I read came to mind. I didn't feel the need to improve my reading ability, but a relatable skill instantly came. I had a crazy idea; why not write a book?

I called my friend Reemus, who has written multiple books, and I asked him for advice on the structure of this book. He asked me for some background information on the idea behind the book and what I wanted the readers to gain. I told him I wanted to write a book that breaks down a range of techniques people can use to enhance their chances of succeeding financially in different aspects of their lives. I wanted the reader to spot economic opportunities in what they put their energy into and understand the best ways to turn their aspirations into reality. Reemus told me to split each technique into chapters, make bullet points for the content of each chapter, then flesh the bullet points out into sentences and paragraphs.

This advice helped me write ten chapters that will allow you to soak up the game from people who have applied the techniques mentioned. This book also gives you the chance to learn from other people's mistakes because I have showcased the actions of people who have misused these techniques. Smart people learn from their mistakes, and wise people learn from other people's mistakes. Thus, I aim to save you time and money by learning from other people's mistakes.

We are currently in the era of YouTube videos and Spotify podcasts, so I ensured that this book has a modern conversational feel. If you don't know what YouTube and Spotify are, this probably means you are reading this book after the year 2062, which means this book was a huge success!

CHAPTER 1

WHERE'S THE MONEY!?

I remember my first time pitching a business idea to an investor. My pitch was passionate, informative, and captivating… if I say so myself. I could sense the investor's delight with what I was saying. I couldn't wait to finish my last sentence to receive shining feedback. However, the three-word response this investor gave me changed my life forever. "WHERE'S THE MONEY!?" I remember feeling confused and startled because I couldn't understand how everything I just said led to such a blunt response. I snapped out of this thinking and realised I had a question to answer. I managed to think on my feet and break down how this business would make money. He seemed satisfied but gave me a week to go away and add financials in my business plan, which detailed the response I had just given.

I called my friend Audrey who works in auditing, for help on the financials and sent the plan to the investor. This led to him showing it to a few more investors, which led to more people coming on board with the project. I learned two things from this. Firstly, always know where the money is coming from when starting a venture. Secondly, when people challenge your response of how you're going to make money, make sure you're prepared, so there are as few holes in your plan as possible.

Social Learning Theory (SLT) suggests humans often carry out behaviour after viewing actions from other humans prior. I was no stranger to this theory because, after this, I began to ask all my friends, "WHERE'S THE MONEY!?" anytime they came to me with a new venture. I found it very funny because they stumbled over their words, and I could tell they felt flustered like I did. After I challenged them, they would go away, then come back in days or weeks with an improved version of their plan, as I did.

Most of the answers to the questions in your head can be found by learning from others' experiences. I want you to learn from the mistakes and successes of the people in this book. This will save you a lot of time, money, and stress if you apply these gems to your life. Speaking of gems, there is one thing I want you to take on board for the rest of your life. When people say, "Money doesn't grow on trees," you should respond, "Maybe you just can't see the trees."

Please expect a blunt response of "What are you talking about?" This is where you say the magic line, "Some people see seeds, and some people see trees".

If you're confused, let me explain. Looking at a seed and envisioning the tree that will grow from it is a skill. It means you can look into the future and see the potential in things. If this tree grows fruit people can eat, this also means it produces fruit you can sell. Hence, the fruit represents the money that is growing on the tree.

Seeing trees instead of seeds is the same thought process you need to execute the "WHERE'S THE MONEY!?" mantra effectively. When you think of an idea or plan, you need to have the foresight to avoid disappointment whilst maximising the chances of a positive result. Anyone can plant the seed, but will the roots have the right environment to get strong, and will the tree be taken care of to produce quality fruit?

We, as humans, have a habit of letting anxiety stop us from achieving our full potential. The thought of failing can abruptly stop us in our stride. My friend Jay, a music producer, makes beats for upcoming local rappers hoping to make it big one day. I believe his beats are better than a lot of beats I hear in the club and on the radio, so I told him to send some of his beats to mainstream rappers as well.

He said he doesn't think that he's at that level yet and doesn't want to let people down, so he wants to work with rappers on his level and try to build with them. Okay… his response was extraordinarily honourable and heart-warming, but "WHERE'S THE MONEY!?" Suppose you think about all the rappers out there compared to those who make it. In that case, you'll soon realise the odds of building sufficient income that relies on upcoming rappers is low.

This doesn't mean he must stop working with upcoming rappers; it just means he could alter his strategy. I showed him the top three songs in a prominent UK rap playlist and asked him to rate the beats out of ten. He gave them a four, six and seven. I asked him to show me the top three beats he has made and to rate them out of ten. He gave them a ten, twenty and one hundred out of ten (his confidence was better than his maths that day).

This is where he started to realise his beats are good enough for mainstream rappers, and he agreed to put some beats aside to send to them. Working with mainstream rappers raises the potential to make higher returns on beats produced because the songs are more likely to receive greater streams, radio plays, licensing deals, etc.

I realised he had a passion for working with upcoming rappers because he related to their raw drive and hunger to make it. This is where I walked him through the leasing business. I broke down how he could earn income from multiple artists using the same beat. For example, if he leased a beat to ten artists for £40 (£400), he could make £300 more than if he exclusively sold the same beat to one artist for £100.

"Your hours need to be expensive" is the cousin of "WHERE'S IS THE MONEY!?" because it simplifies every action we take into monetary terms. In the leasing example above, Jay might have spent three hours making a beat and was able to lease it to ten people to earn £400. That would mean he earned roughly £133.33 per hour, making that beat (£400 / three hours). However, if he sold the beat to one person for £100, he would have only made roughly £33.33 an hour (£100 / three hours).

Let's dive into "Your hours need to be expensive" a little more. I was having a conversation with my friend Tosan. We were debating if our time at university was worth it. We started to compare the entrepreneurs we knew to people who went to university we also knew. We concluded that entrepreneurs who were earning more than university graduates charged higher prices for their products/services than competitors in their industry. For example, most barbers charge under £20 to trim Afro-Caribbean hair. However, the high-earning barbers we knew charged £100 for their haircuts and built up their names by trimming footballers, influencers, and musicians.

Therefore, when we compared the university graduates to the barbers making £20 per haircut, they made considerably more. However, when we compared them to the barbers charging £100 per haircut, most of the university graduates made much less (annually).

Just think about it… If the £20 barber trims eight people in a day, they will make £160. If the £100 barber trims eight people in a day, they will make £800. That made Tosan and me dig deeper into "Your hours need to be expensive." The £20 barber and £100 barber are practically doing the same job, but one makes £640 more than the other in a day.

The £100 barber probably got told to "work smart, not hard" at some point. He spent time building up his connections with people who had strong networks made up of wealthy and popular individuals. Thus, he saw the value of networking and used this as a separator to ensure his hours were expensive.

This is just Branding 101 because we all know that a Gucci T-shirt doesn't cost £900 to make, and people will still pay £900 to buy it with no complaints or questions. In contrast, people will complain and question an unknown designer who was selling a similar T-shirt at a pop-up store for £100. The difference is the customer's perception of the product because both T-shirts could have been made from the same fabric.

Therefore, you should focus on your personal, product, or service's perception because it can be a crucial differentiator when it comes to requesting a higher salary or setting a higher price. Try to add to your qualifications, network, and knowledge before diving into a job or business because giving yourself a head start can be priceless.

The evil cousin of "WHERE'S THE MONEY!?" is greed. It's good to think about how you can monetise situations and opportunities, but sometimes people/companies take it too far. Lumosity is an online program that provides games that claim to develop your problem-solving, memory, processing speed, etc. Lumosity released a "brain-training" memory game targeted at the older generation.

Many studies have shown that humans live longer year on year, so more people are likely to suffer from Alzheimer's and dementia. Thus, many people from the elder demographic felt as though Lumosity's brain training would be fun and mentally beneficial due to the nature of Lumosity's advertising.

Multiple scientists tested the claims of Lumosity's brain training. They found they had little effect compared to the mental improvements Lumosity promised in their advertising.

This was distasteful to many people because Lumosity was charging $299.95 for subscriptions.

Lumosity was accused of taking advantage of consumer fears and making false promises about the capabilities of their games by US Federal Investigators. Lumosity was sanctioned $2 million to settle fraudulent claim charges and $50 million for harming consumers.

Lumosity probably noticed a gap in the market for brain-stimulating games for the growing elder population and thought, "WHERE'S THE MONEY!?" However, greed seeped into the equation when they used false advertising along with a high subscription fee to maximise their profits, built from a disingenuous buzz.

Lumosity could have stuck to creating games that "exercise the brain" but got greedy when they realised they could make more money by exaggerating the capabilities of their games. When using the "WHERE'S THE MONEY!?" mantra, always have good ethics at the centre of your actions.

Another thing you should watch out for with the "WHERE'S THE MONEY!?" mantra is excitement. Have you been in a situation where the excitement of your idea was sweeter than when you got what you were fantasising about? If so, you know excitement can lead to bad decision making because it clouds your judgement.

Money and sex are two things that can lead to bad decisions due to excitement, but in this book, we will only be diving into money! I nearly made a bad decision with money due to excitement. I spent months working with two investors on a project I had previously pitched to them. We spent ages going back and forth with the contractual terms, and we had finally agreed on the final edit of the contract.

I was excited because the gruelling process was finally concluding, and my project was going to be brought to life.

However, on the evening we agreed to sign, the two investors told me they wanted us all to have equal voting rights. Let's dive into this… So, two business partners wanted me to agree to split the voting rights in my company equally with them?

If I let excitement take over, I would agree to minority power in my own company. This means on the first day of signing that contract; the two business partners could vote me out of the business because of their two-thirds majority stake. This would have been a clear example of a hostile takeover. The two business partners could argue they would never vote me out of my company, but one thing undeniable is power. They would always know they could collude to go against any major moves that I want to make or deny any objections I make to their proposals.

I was happy and sad after this happened. I was obviously sad I didn't get to push forward with the project, but I was glad I didn't let the lure of the money cloud my judgement. Don't let excitement lead to overzealous decision making because you can't plant your seed in every soil.

WHERE'S THE MONEY!? - Theoretical Example: - Makeup artist (MUA)

Sarah worked for MAC as a makeup artist for the past three years inside their Selfridges store. She has a strong relationship with her clients, and they keep recommending her to start her own MUA business. MAC has strict guidelines that state "employees are forbidden from discussing their personal ventures with our customers." Sarah decides to take the risk and ignore the guidelines set by MAC. When Sarah received positive feedback from a client, she would give them her business card and offer to charge them a cheaper rate if they came to her personally.

Sarah converted her gazebo in her garden to a beauty lab, then shortly after, she was booked up for the next two months.

Patricia was one of her clients from MAC who recommended that Sarah should go solo.

Patricia said to Sarah, "To succeed in life, you need to see the potential in things and then execute effectively." Patricia added, "Some people see seeds whilst I see trees. I saw the potential in you so, I'm happy you took my advice, and your business is doing well."

Sarah replied, "I spent a lot of money converting this gazebo into a beauty lab; the quality of makeup products my clients are used to using are expensive, and my prices are low. My costs are very high, and I'm not making enough revenue to break even."

Patricia paused before answering with a soft murmur, "Where's the money?"

Sarah said, "Huh, pardon?"

Patricia responded, "WHERE'S THE MONEY!? It's wonderful you used your talent to go solo, but did you spend enough time working out the numbers?"

Sarah went silent.

Patricia continued, "Your customers were happy to pay MAC's price originally, so set your price at that amount. Explain the price drop was a welcome offer. Also, this gazebo can fit at least two other beauticians. Ask around; see if any hairdressers or nail technicians are looking for a place to work."

Sarah said, "Wow, how did you think of all that so quickly? Those are amazing ideas."

Patricia replied, "The trick is to turn your issues and what you already have into money. You had a price issue, so raise it. You spent money on this gazebo; well, make the most out of it by utilising the space."

Patricia continued, "The other issue you mentioned was the cost of the products. This issue could be solved by the price increase and the rent collecting. The extra money you will make will cover this cost, so you'll finally be in the green."

I hope you have soaked up all the game from Patricia and me, and you're ready to use the "WHERE'S THE MONEY!?" mantra to take in the rest of this book.

CHAPTER 2

BEING LAUGHED AT

One of my friends, Hafeez, sent me a video of himself rapping on WhatsApp and challenged me to respond. I decided to give it a go and channel myself back to secondary school when I used to "clash" people lyrically. Hafeez really liked the response I sent back and said I should make it into a full song. I laughed and asked if he was joking, and he said, "No, send it to the rest of the guys and see what they think." Fast forward two weeks; I'm sitting in a studio with my friends about to record the song because they all liked the initial video.

This was something totally out of my comfort zone, but anyone who knows me knows I'm not scared to try most things. When I put the song out, I realised many people wrote it off before listening. I was probably laughed at and asked, "Are you serious!?" the most I've been in my life. Many of these people eventually gave me good feedback after listening to the song. Some still found it funny after giving it a good review.

This was a pivotal period because I learned a life lesson. There's going to be people who laugh at you and behind your back when you try something new. Humans find it hard to accept a new image of other people due to the set image they originally had in their head. Additionally, some people project their own insecurities on others, so they will try to stop you from trying new things because they're not brave enough to do this themselves.

When Dwayne "The Rock" Johnson started to act in films, people found it funny that a former wrestler and someone who was that physically imposing in size could be taken seriously as an actor. The irony is, to be a top WWE wrestler, you have to be a good actor and entertainer, so he already had crossover skills. Consequently, in 2018, Dwayne "The Rock" Johnson became the highest-paid actor since *Forbes* created their list over twenty years prior ($124 million).

Many people let the embarrassment of being laughed at stop them from achieving their goals and ambitions. This leads to people getting boxed off into categories and not fulfilling their potential. If you want to discover new talents and fulfil your potential, you need to battle through the embarrassment of being laughed at.

Did you know there is a word for the fear of being laughed at? It's gelotophobia.

Research has shown that gelotophobia falls under the "social phobia" category. It details the behaviour of people who have a severe fear of being laughed at. Gelotophobia is often caused by bullying in adolescence years and can lead to social withdrawal.

The most extreme cases of gelotophobia show people being triggered by the laughter of strangers in the same vicinity because they assume people are making them the butt of a joke. Even if you don't suffer from an extreme case of gelotophobia, you will still be able to see that people prevent showcasing their new ideas or abilities in fear of being laughed at. One of the ways you can reduce this fear is by putting yourself in the shoes of the people who were laughing at you.

Why are they actually laughing at your new idea or ability?

Is it because they are not brave enough to take risks themselves, so they put down others to make themselves feel better?

Is it because they got laughed at when they tried to step outside their own box, so they are now doing the same thing to you (social learning theory)?

Do they actually think your new behaviour is silly?

Even if they think your new behaviour is "silly," you should never let someone else's opinion stop you from doing what you feel destined to do. If you never try something new, you will never know your calling in life, so don't let other people block your blessings.

Another way you can overcome the fear of being laughed at is by joining in on the joke but biting back subtly. If your friends think it's funny you want to start a YouTube channel on yoga because you are physically out of shape, you should respond:

"Yeah, you're right; people are going to find it so funny when they see me in my fitness gear struggling to touch my toes, haha. But I think I will have a niche audience of people who are also in my position and would love encouragement from someone similar to them. So, I'm sure my YouTube channel will grow."

In the example above, you can see the power was taken back when you show you can also laugh at yourself (them laughing doesn't affect you). You also made them feel silly for not noticing there is potential in this venture because they were being narrow-minded. This approach is much more effective than lashing out due to their laughter or telling them about the bigger picture in a defensive tone.

David Icke is a controversial conspiracy theorist who has made many outlandish statements that have been laughed at and ridiculed. He received much media attention for claiming that shape-shifting reptilian aliens rule Earth. He believes that these aliens can disguise themselves in human form to gain political power to control humans.

David Icke has been laughed at, vilified, and even banned from Twitter for his views on various topics. No matter whether you agree with David Icke, you should be able to admire his ability to voice his opinion, even though he knows he'll be laughed at. David has a famous quote: "The greatest prison people live in is the fear of what people think."

David's quote is powerful because he states that the mental prison is more dire than any physical prison. This is interesting because many prisoners remain in good spirits by saying, "They can lock up my body but not my mind" or "My body isn't free, but my mind will always be free." David's quote coincides with these two quotes because the prisoners are grateful to still have mental freedom; however, David believes people are not mentally free when they let the fear of what people think control their actions.

Okay… you may be thinking, "Great quote, but do you really expect me to listen to an alien conspiracy theorist?" and my answer is yes! We can all learn from people who think outside of the box. We don't need to believe what they say, but we can take note of their fearlessness and add elements of this into our own lives.

I have explained why you shouldn't let other people's laughter stop you from moving ahead with your ideas; however, you should also be wary of switching roles with people who laugh at other people's ideas. Thus, the other side of the coin is not laughing at other people when they try something new. The downside of doing this is you will subconsciously be telling yourself not to take such risks in your own future, and people you laugh at won't be motivated when you need their help in the future.

Kevin Eastman and Peter Laird created a comic book called *Teenage Mutant Ninja Turtles* (TMNT) in 1984. They linked up with a licensing agent, Mark Freedman, who saw potential in the comic and wanted to turn the characters into toys. Mark pitched the TMNT characters to multiple toy companies and heard "no" numerous times.

He was told that the idea was stupid, no kids would want to play with green toys, and was laughed at in several meetings. After being rejected by toy giants such as Mattel, Hasbro, and LJN, Mark Freedman managed to secure a deal with a toy company called Playmates, which were based in Hong Kong. Playmates worked tirelessly with the TMNT brand and even created cartoons and films to enhance the brand. In 1990 alone, they sold 100 million toys after building a globally impactful brand for TMNT.

Mattel, Hasbro, and LJN had huge regrets about not taking TMNT seriously when it was first pitched to them. These companies spent many years struggling to create products to compete with the considerable market share TMNT had. Therefore, you shouldn't write off new ideas too quickly because you're not giving yourself enough time to process the potential of something that could become a market leader.

Kevin Eastman and Peter Laird came up with the TMNT concept, and some people thought their comic book was silly. However, Mark Freedman believed in it and helped take their comic to the next level by bringing toys, cartoons, live-action series, and films into the equation. Thus, it only takes one person to believe in your "crazy idea" to turn it into a success. One believer can create millions of other believers, so you don't necessarily have to do all the convincing yourself. Just believe in what you are bringing to the table, and your confidence will eventually convince the right people.

Social media has taken being laughed at to a whole new level. Strangers will comment on anything you show. You are likely to receive discouragement from multiple people outside of your network. This can be more difficult than being laughed at by people you know or companies you reached out to. When people you know laugh at you, it can hurt, but you can rationalise it as them "hating" or not being used to you doing this new thing. Additionally, when you pitch to a company or ask for funds from an investor, you always know there is a possibility of hearing no or them not understanding your idea, so you prepare yourself for this in advance.

However, social media discouragement can come out of nowhere, so it is harder to prepare yourself for and rationalise it. You must realise that you are susceptible to discouragement when you release a new product or service or announce a career change. Platforms such as Twitter can be highly toxic because some people log on to discourage other people in the hope of gaining likes, retweets, and followers. They may not dislike what you have released but spotted an opportunity to grow their online presence by putting down yours.

Before you press upload, tweet, post, etc., please prepare yourself for discouragement. Write down the worst comments you can imagine people could say about your new idea. Make funny jokes about it for your own amusement. To keep balance, you should also write a list of all the positive comments you could imagine people would say and the potential success you can achieve. Read over what you have written and only post once you feel desensitised to the negative comments you have written.

Mentally preparing yourself for adverse scenarios can reduce the shock factor of negative situations. Shock leads to your mind going blank and not efficiently dealing with the task you have at hand most competently. If writing down negative comments isn't having the impact you were aiming for, then ask a friend you trust to read these out loud to you.

Hearing negative comments from an external voice can help you process them better and accept the potential discouragement to come. Please ensure your friend reads out the positive comments after the negative comments because you should have a positive mindset and positive thoughts when posting on social media.

Historically, people have been comfortable criticising and laughing at celebrity mishaps. Still, social media has made it a norm for regular people to receive this treatment. Positive thoughts are needed, but you should always prepare yourself for the possibility of a negative reaction.

I'll let you into a secret… I had finished this chapter already, but I came back to add this section after a conversation I had just had with my friend Tosan. I told him about this book, and he said that his Sunday service reminded him of the "Being Laughed At" chapter.

A few years ago, Tosan invited a few of his other friends and me to watch his baptism ceremony. Tosan gave a captivating speech in front of a large audience on his reasons for getting baptised. That day, I noticed Tosan's public speaking ability, so I told him I could see him being a really impactful pastor if he puts his mind to it. Fast forward to the Sunday that had just passed; I watched Tosan's first service, where he preached to the church as a trainee pastor.

The strangest thing happened. I randomly kept giggling to myself when Tosan was preaching because his facial expressions and passion in the way he delivered his point reminded me of when we had debates about football or music. Seeing Tosan in this new light was weird, even though I envisioned him being pastor years back. This showed me that even I am susceptible to laughing at people trying something new. I found it amusing seeing a friend I grew up with, in a completely different light.

I told Tosan he did really well, and he thanked me for believing in him before he even started his journey as a pastor. I told him it was strange to see him in that role, and his facial expressions and delivery made me laugh. I explained the "being laughed at" concept in this book, and he said it's something he does himself when adjusting to change, even though he doesn't mean offence. It was nice to see my friend excel at something new, have him appreciate my support, and understand it would take time for people to adjust. However, being laughed at won't always be such a smooth process, especially when there is malice behind it, so you should always go into a new action expecting it. As mentioned previously, preparation is key, so always account for positive and negative reactions from your peers and from strangers.

Laughter is good for the soul, so when people laugh at you, be honoured; you're priceless to their well-being.

CHAPTER 3

POWER OF THE VILLIAN

I'm sure you have heard the phrase "Bad press is good press." Donald Trump, Kanye West, and Piers Morgan all have something in common. They could get people who oppose their views to give them free promotions and put money in their pockets. The secret to this ability relates to the phrase "confidence over competence." Donald Trump's perceived confidence allowed him to qualify for arguably the highest job position on earth (US President) without prior experience.

Look… I'm not telling you to follow the ideologies of Donald Trump, Kanye West, and Piers Morgan, but there is a lot to learn from them. To break moulds or gain a first-mover advantage, you must understand you are shifting the norms of society. This can cause an uproar from the majority, which you must be willing to face. The uproar is in the same family as being laughed at (discussed in chapter 2) because you are put in a position where you must re-evaluate the actions you have just taken.

Kanye West got his big break by being invited to make beats and produce music for Jay-Z; however, this wasn't satisfying enough for him. Kanye wanted to be a rapper but was constantly laughed at by Jay-Z and his manager, Dame Dash. Kanye didn't dress like a rapper, and his music wasn't considered "gangster" or "street," so it's no surprise he was laughed at.

Kanye was brave enough to battle through being laughed at and showed early signs of the "power of the villain." In packed studio rooms with Jay-Z and his entourage, Kanye used to abruptly stop producing and then stand on tables and rap his lyrics a capella. Jay-Z and his entourage used to hate when Kanye did this, but the confidence packaged with his lyrics eventually made them view his lyrics as competent.

Kanye kept repeating this behaviour until his peers started to get used to him as a rapper rather than being "just a producer." Kanye used the repetition and consistency (chapter 9) tool to convince his peers to see his vision. Once he won the approval of Jay-Z and his entourage, Kanye's confidence went up another level, which made him feel unstoppable as a rapper. The fearlessness to use the power of the villain tool is arguably one reason why Kanye West received twenty-one Grammy Awards.

Speaking of awards… arguably, Kanye's most infamous moment came when he interrupted nineteen-year-old Taylor Swift's MTV Best Female Video award acceptance speech to say that Beyonce should have won the award instead. Many people felt that this was hugely disrespectful and made Kanye a villain in their eyes. Kanye realised this and used the hate from critics to fuel him throughout his career.

When Kanye was trying to break into the fashion industry, he realised he faced many nay-sayers, like he did when he wanted to be a rapper. Luckily, he had faced this task before and already had a blueprint. Kanye didn't stand on tables this time or randomly start rapping in packed rooms. He decided to schedule interviews with some of the biggest interview platforms and passionately called out all the people/companies he felt were blocking or didn't believe in him.

This began to ruffle feathers with some of the public, who thought he was acting entitled and arrogant. It also ruffled the feathers of the people and companies he called out and heightened his status as a villain in many people's eyes.

The most infamous interview Kanye had was with the presenter Sway, where he compared himself to Andy Warhol, William Shakespeare, Walt Disney, Nike, and Google. He said he's the "number-one impactful artist of this generation". He said he needs investment from people to fund his vision. Sway asked him why he couldn't fund his vision himself, and Kanye responded with the famous line "HOW SWAY!?," which went on to be a popular phrase during that time. Even though the phrase was humorous and famous, many people still didn't like the brute manner Kanye was speaking to Sway, which, again, furthered his reputation as a villain.

Kanye originally had a deal with Nike for his "Yeezy" sneakers, which was a big success at the time. Nike wasn't prepared to submit to Kanye's ownership and control demands, so he publicly criticised Nike. It was only a matter of time before Nike's fiercest competitor, Adidas, began to circle and made a deal with Kanye. Consequently, Bank of America valued the sneaker side of the Yeezy brand at as much as $3 billion in 2020. That same year, GAP, Inc. announced they partnered up with Kanye to create new apparel: the Yeezy Gap line.

Kanye wasn't getting what he wanted from companies like Nike, so he made this information publicly known. Kanye knew he could be perceived as arrogant, ignorant, and rude; however, he had played this game before, so he knew how to win. You may not think Kanye's approach fits in with your morals, and that is totally understandable. However, what you should take from Kanye is he was willing to step outside of the norms of society in terms of how we "should" behave. Also, when you are working with huge companies such as Nike, you should always value your own worth, and you should be willing to leave and seek new opportunities, even if that risks your current situation.

This chapter isn't advocating you to throw your toys out of the pram when things aren't going well in your life. This chapter is to make you aware of alternative tactics to the ones you may usually use. Be bold enough to showcase your talent and skills in unorthodox environments. Be brave enough to let people know what you can bring to the table and that you are willing to partner up with new partners if they don't believe in you enough. There's no need to scream in people's faces. You should speak with assertiveness and confidence and not let people convince you that your confidence is arrogance.

I have helped someone execute the power of the villain tactic, which eventually led to millions of views, business opportunities, and thousands of fans. I am good friends with Paul "The Provider" Bridges, who told me he was offered the chance to be on a new reality show called *Blue Therapy*. He was asked to act as the boyfriend of a well-known influencer called Chioma.

Paul is an affluent funny guy, but he's well-mannered and generally a nice guy. However, I knew he would only be known as "Chioma's boyfriend" if he didn't overpower her character. I told him about the power of the villain, and we even went as far as to plan out some of the storylines. Once Paul bought into the power of the villain, he unlocked another level of his acting ability. He got into character brilliantly when the time came for filming and eventually became the biggest star on the show.

Paul was ignorant, bold, outlandish, cheeky, arrogant, and shocking. These are prominent characteristics of many villains and arguably the same characteristics Kanye West is infamous for. *The Guardian* described Paul as the "breakout star (or villain)." *The Metro* documented Paul as "rude" and "the most problematic cast member."

National newspaper coverage rubberstamped the magnitude of Paul's power of the villain tactic. *Blue Therapy* amassed over twelve million views and helped kickstart Paul's notoriety. Paul has received a blue tick on social media, interviewed with significant publications, worked with elite brands on partnership deals, and sold out of the products and services he offered on his website. You may be thinking: How can someone who is so badly behaved be rewarded for their actions?

In my secondary/high school, the kids who were worst behaved and had the worst grades would get taken out on school trips no one else got invited to. They used to go quad bike riding and get taken to adventure parks during school times. As the years went by, I realised this was always done when the school had Ofsted or inspectors around. Thus, the school removed all the "bad" kids from the premises to avoid poor Ofsted ratings: clever and crafty if you ask me.

The school could have simply taken them to do extra classes outside of school or brought in an external tutor. Still, they decided to reward them for their bad behaviour. This is a strange human characteristic that doesn't get discussed much. The Joker is one of the most famous fictional villains. He is known for being psychotic, blowing up hospitals and torturing people. Why did the *Joker* movie (2019) become the highest-grossing R rated film of all time? The same reason Paul's behaviour on *Blue Therapy* led to success.

Humans have a moral compass of what is good and bad. Some people would say, "When you do good, you are loved, and when you do bad, you are hated." However, others would argue there is a thin line between love and hate. Therefore, many villains start off being hated, then end up being loved. People begin to see rudeness as humour and malice as being misunderstood. Once you have seen the worst in someone, there is no other ceiling; the only thing that can happen is you begin to accept them and start to look for the good in them. This is the sweet spot where villains begin to turn haters into fans.

Another reason people love the villain is that they see characteristics in the villain that they see in themselves. Academic Rebecca Krause (PhD) stated that people who are tricky are drawn to the Joker (from Batman). People who feel as ambitious and intellectual as Voldemort (from Harry Potter) would be drawn to him. Psychologists Keen et al. (2018) found that people are drawn to villains because they identify with their personalities and are fascinated watching the villain do things they may fantasize about. Thus, there would be men who watched Paul boldly tell Chioma that he didn't like her cooking who have fantasized about telling their wife the same thing!

Even though the power of the villain tactic can lead to success, it is clearly the riskiest tactic discussed in this book. We live in an era of people being "cancelled" for things that were okay the previous day. Also, you need to be able to have extremely thick skin to hear constant backlash to most things you say and do. Villains have times when they hit their limit and cannot take the backlash anymore; Piers Morgan is an excellent example of this.

Piers Morgan is known for being a villain because he is infamous for being an antagonist and someone who crosses the line. Piers used to be the editor of the *Daily Mirror*. During his tenure, the paper was accused of hacking the phones of victims, celebrities, and politicians for information to be used in news reports. This arguably set the tone for Piers being a villain, and he seemed to publicly run with this persona.

Piers took part in the first *Celebrity* series of *The Apprentice,* which was hosted by Donald Trump in the US. This show put people through their paces by testing their business acumen in various challenges. Piers went on to win the show, and many people felt that Donald Trump chose him because they are birds of the same feathers. Piers was arrogant and was willing to step over people to get what he wanted, which are characteristics of a villain.

An excellent example of the overuse of the power of the villain tactic came when Piers began to voice his opinions about Meghan Markle. Piers divided public opinion by continuously calling out Meghan for bringing shame to the Royal Family. Meghan expressed that her mental health had been affected by the bullying, racism, and lack of care from the media and "the firm" (the people in charge of the management of the Royal Family). Piers had some supporters who believed Meghan was playing the "sympathy card." However, other people strongly disagreed with him. They felt he had a personal vendetta against Meghan and a lack of respect for mental health issues.

Piers began to do daily rants on his Twitter account and on *Good Morning Britain* (a TV show he co-presented) about Meghan. He became obsessive in many people's eyes. He was determined to "prove" his point and tried to use the same tactics he used on *The Apprentice*: by walking over anyone in his way. However, some of the people he was trying to walk over were advocates of mental health issues, which had become a huge movement at the time, so the people he began to offend grew bigger and bigger. He also began to offend people from the Black Lives Matter movement because many people felt that he was dismissive of the racism claims Meghan made about the media and "the firm."

The boiling point came when Piers' *Good Morning Britain* colleague, Alex Beresford, called him out on live TV by defending Meghan profusely and went as far as calling Piers "pathetic." Piers had previously done an interview where he said Meghan left a meet-up to meet Prince Harry. Many people felt as though that's where his personal vendetta began. Thus, Alex accused Piers of having a personal issue with Meghan because she cut him off when he aimed to date her romantically in the past. Piers angrily stormed off the set and said, "OK, I'm done with this; sorry, no, can't do this." You can see from Piers' reaction that he hit his limit and had taken the power of the villain tactic too far. Alex arguably triggered Piers by saying some truths he wasn't prepared to face. It was very ironic because, like other villains, Piers is known for "dishing it out" but wasn't prepared to take it when the shoe was on the other foot.

That same day, ITV, who broadcasts *Good Morning Britain,* announced they had parted ways with Piers. This came on the back of over 40,000 Ofcom complaints on Piers' behaviour when speaking about Meghan. Piers had lost the respect of many members of the public and his job because he took the power of the villain tactic too far.

You may be thinking, "What's the point of using the power of the villain tactic if I can lose respect and my job!?" Like with most things in life, you should use them in moderation. Too much of most things lead to tragedy, and you should only use certain tactics in certain situations. If Piers had simply explained his opinion on Meghan and moved on, the public could have listened and moved on. However, he was commentating on Meghan daily. He even went as far as citing her relationship with her father as "evidence" of her dysfunctions.

Piers could have acknowledged that her mental health may have been affected or she felt mistreated due to her race. Instead, he was extremely dismissive of both. He even accused her of lying about her mental health issues, which is extremely triggering for people going through those issues.

I mentioned above that certain tactics should only be used in certain situations, and I think Kanye West realised this long ago. Kanye didn't start rapping for Jay Z the first time he met him; he built up his credit as a producer to show his value initially. Once he felt like an asset, he took advantage of this by bringing something else to the table. He built up his confidence over time and gave Jay Z time to grow to like him.

Psychologists Keen et al. (2018) found that our perception of other people changes when we learn about their circumstances, so we begin to emphasise with them over time. Empathy fosters the environment for the sweet spot, where people start to become drawn to the villain.

You should always aim to be a light in other people's lives and uplift them as well as yourself. Contemplate the option of using bothersome tactics to get to the level you desire. This doesn't have to become a characteristic or personality trait, but sometimes you have to get your hands dirty. Think about "successful" fictional and non-fictional villains and take elements of their characteristics to push forward your own goals in life. One characteristic most villains share is the ability to go against the norm, which is a vital characteristic of an innovator.

The only people more celebrated than villains are heroes. There are more people in life trying to be a hero, so your chances of success solely following that blueprint could be slim. If you decide to dabble into the traits of a villain, make sure you have your morals at the centre of your actions to prevent you from going too far.

The Joker movie (2019) earned over $1 billion in the box office; do you really think a film about Robin could do such numbers?

CHAPTER 4

USING STEREOTYPES TO YOUR ADVANTAGE

People often complain about being stereotyped because they feel it leads to prejudice and disadvantages. I believe people can use their stereotypes to their advantage if they become self-aware of how other people perceive them. You can type "stereotypes" next to something that describes you in Google to find out your stereotypes. For example, if you consider yourself as being short in height and you're a male, you could search "short guy stereotypes." Most of the things you find will be offensive, but once you get past that, you can get a rough idea of how the world judges you. This will raise your self-awareness levels, leading to you using your stereotypes to your advantage. Let me tell you about a time where my stereotype gave me an advantage and contributed to a successful project.

I remember being at university, and one of my friends told me she wears wigs, and I bantered her all day. She explained how she started making, selling and sending them in the post. I was shocked about all of this and felt as though I had discovered a big secret. My university campus was like being in the *Big Brother* house because you learn so much about people and especially the hidden habits of the opposite sex. I noticed the

Black girls with the best-kept hair wore wigs; it was easier to maintain.

After a while, it became a norm as wig tutorials moved to Instagram and YouTube. Black women began to be unapologetic by discussing "wig life" more openly on Twitter. It used to be something that was hidden and not spoken about due to the fear of judgement from men and other races.

After I graduated and began my career, I checked in with my friend Sharon to ask how her graduate job was going. She told me some of her work stories that involved lies about her hair. She told me she tells her colleagues she's going for a haircut the day before she switches to a short wig, so her change in the wig isn't alarming. She would then wear the short wig for a fair amount of time because if she went from a short to a long wig, her colleagues would become curious about the miraculous growth. She explained to me that black women already deal with a lot of discriminatory undertones in the office, so she didn't want to bring additional negative attention to herself.

I found this very intriguing, so I began to ask more women if they face this issue. There was so much passion in the voices of the women I spoke to for a question I initially thought was trivial. They all voluntarily gave me personal and emotional responses, which I didn't know I was provoking.

These women had stories that took me on a journey from what styles they did when they were younger and their development in terms of knowing what products to use to maintain their hair as they got more knowledgeable. They also spoke about the pressures of "fitting in" at school, work, and society, without ever really having a voice. This was when I realised that the topic was huge but undiscussed.

I had the idea to turn this into a documentary, even though I had never made a production in my life. I'm the type of person who likes to execute my ideas because I feel as though it goes to waste if I don't. However, there was one big problem.

How would a heterosexual black male succeed in producing a documentary on the hair experiences of black women?

If he uses his stereotype to his advantage, obviously!

The stereotype of a heterosexual black male doesn't match up with the profile of someone many people would expect to produce content about the beauty industry and hair experiences of women.

When I began to reach out to potential cast members, many of them were intrigued that a guy was willing to raise awareness about their struggles. Unintentionally, this became my USP when pitching the idea to the cast members because they instantly saw the potential the documentary had by being hosted by a guy. One of the cast members was very shocked when she arrived for filming because she was expecting me to be a woman. I only spoke to her via email, so I'm not sure if she thought "Ish" was short for Ishia or something!?

When I released the trailer for the documentary on Twitter and Instagram, I received numerous comments and direct messages from women who said it was amazing to see a guy take on such a vast topic concerning women. Using my stereotype to my advantage was something I did unintentionally. Still, it was a significant factor that led to the documentary's success. *Black Girl Hair: Embarrassed, Proud or Shy* was received exceptionally well by the viewers and was written about in press articles. I was also given the opportunity to collaborate with some big brands in the beauty industry due to the documentary's success.

Alex Scott (MBE) is an ex-professional football player who played in the English Women's Premier League, in which she won the trophy five times with Arsenal. She also represented the England Women's national team and won a bronze medal in the FIFA Women's World Cup in 2015. Alex is a household name in women's football but wasn't known as much amongst the fans of men's football.

In 2018, Alex gained some exposure to the fans of men's football when she did punditry for the BBC at the Men's 2018 FIFA World Cup. Alex was the first female pundit at a FIFA World Cup in the BBC's history. There were people on social media who began to discredit Alex as a pundit, stating she only got the job to fill a quota. Alex was getting judged for her gender before people had time to even appreciate her punditry skills.

In 2020, Sky Sports let go of some male pundits who had been at the company for many years and who were popular ex-footballers. Phil Thompson, Matt Le Tissier, and Charlie Nicolas were all let go, and Alex Scott was hired by Sky Sports in the same period. This led to backlash on social media, where people cited her ethnicity and her gender as the reasons she was hired.

Former Arsenal Men's footballer Ian Wright spoke out against these people on social media and said, "The racism is going through the roof today." He added, "Because a black person or woman might get the opportunity to do this job, why are people upset?" He then described Alex as "one of the best-prepared pundits out there, easily."

Alex was ridiculed for being a woman pursuing a career that was dominated by men and was also given abuse for being black. However, the stereotypes about her gender and ethnicity became her differentiator because they made her unique.

Alex's bravery to battle through the abuse led to her being celebrated as a pioneer for female pundits. Alex's fine performances as a pundit were able to open the door for other female pundits. In 2021, ITV hired Chelsea Women's football manager Emma Hayes to be a pundit for the European Championships. She was named the number-one pundit in OLBG's Commentator rankings research.

Alex wasn't only talented at her job; she was also a black woman, which made her stand out amongst her colleagues, predominantly white males. This made Alex distinctive and could have been part of why EA Sports selected Alex as one of the commentators for their Iconic game FIFA 22.

Please don't think I am discrediting Alex's ability as a pundit and commentator. I said her ethnicity and gender may have contributed to her being selected by EA Sports. I agree with Ian Wright because I think that she is "one of the best-prepared pundits out there." I also believe change always ruffles feathers at first, and once it is accepted, people get behind it quickly because they don't want to be called out. Initially, people used lazy stereotypes, such as assuming a woman wouldn't be clued up about football, and black pundits aren't as logical as their white counterparts. However, they eventually realised Alex was talented at her job, so more opportunities naturally came. Her ethnicity and gender became bonuses rather than hindrances.

Award-winning fashion designer Kerby Jean-Raymond is the founder of the brand Pyer Moss (est. 2013), which has been described as a "luxury streetwear brand." Kerby has also been listed on the *Forbes* 30 Under 30 list for his achievements with Pyer Moss. Kerby took part in a Netflix documentary called *The Remix – Hip Hop x Fashion*. In this documentary, he said, "At Pyer Moss, I didn't really want anyone knowing that I was Black. Like, the first year or so, I hid my face. I didn't do interviews."

Kerby knew that his brand may not be considered as high fashion if people knew a black person was behind it. He felt that brands considered as high fashion by the public are run by white people. Kerby knew the stereotypes attached to black fashion brands was the opposite of high fashion. Cheap, tacky, and fads are some of the stereotypes, which is not what Kerby aimed to be associated with.

Kerby is an example of someone who felt as though their stereotype was too detrimental to try to use to their advantage. Kerby cited Misa Hylton (who styled Mary J Blige, Lil Kim, Aaliyah, and Missy Elliot) as an example of a black fashion designer who would have been given more opportunities from publications such as *Vogue* if she wasn't black. Hence, he didn't want to follow the same fate as his predecessors.

Kerby began to feel like he wasn't being true to himself by hiding his appearance as a black man. He was touched by the killings of young black boys in America, such as Trayvon Martin, Eric Garner, and Michael Brown, so he wanted to do something to make a difference. Kerby decided to reach out to the families of these victims and recorded interviews of them describing how the killing and loss made them feel. He also put together footage of police brutality towards black people and put it all together as a montage. Kerby put together a fashion runway show with clothes inspired by freedom and the fight against brutality towards black people. He also showed the video montage I mentioned above throughout the show.

The rawness of the videos shocked many audience members and made them extremely uncomfortable. After the show, Pyer Moss lost over $100,000 worth of business, and many of their biggest clients dropped them. Kerby said that this sent him into depression, and he even received death threats from white nationalists. Kerby was living in regret because he knew that if he just carried on being anonymous and hadn't revealed that he was black or fighting for black issues, this would never have happened.

Kerby was close to closing down Pyer Moss after the turmoil of the fashion show, but this all changed when he received an encouraging call from multi-Grammy Award-winning singer Erykah Badu. She told him the message he is putting out there is important, and it doesn't matter how his clothes make people feel because the movement he created travels beyond fashion. This conversation, along with garment orders from other celebrities, gave Kerby the motivation to continue. Kerby used the money earned from these new orders to put together more fashion shows along the same vein.

Kerby's fashion shows began to gather media attention over time because he pioneered something that was very raw and uncut within the fashion industry. Publications such as *The New York Times*, *Vogue,* and *Elle* praised his bravery, creativity, and foresight. Kerby won the CFDA/Vogue Fashion Fund for emerging American design talent in 2018. Kerby initially thought being black was a hindrance to Misa Hylton being featured in publications like *Vogue*. Ironically, he won an award and was featured in *Vogue* for showcasing black issues as a black designer. You can argue that "times change," but I would argue that Kerby's bravery contributed heavily to this change. Rather than him hiding behind his stereotype, he eventually used it as a differentiator to make him unique within the fashion industry.

Dress up your perceived weaknesses in the same clothes you dress your strengths in because people will gradually forget their preconceptions.

CHAPTER 5

GO WHERE YOU'RE APPRECIATED

Xenophobia is the fear or dislike of someone outside of your demographic. Most people would say "no" if you asked them if they were racist or prejudiced. However, they would probably admit to feeling more comfortable socialising with people from their own demographic(s). When people behave prejudiced, they harm themselves and others because being narrow-minded blocks the foresight of potential opportunities.

Suppose you're an aspiring football player and your family always spoke negatively towards Italians. In that case, you may reject the opportunity to play in Italy. However, your skillset may be best suited to Italian leagues. Still, now you have missed out on a massive opportunity because of xenophobia. It is always best to be open-minded when opportunities arise because the place for you to fulfil your potential may be outside of your current location.

Music video director Flex God Daps realised the UK rap industry had low financial investment and was in its infancy stages in comparison to the US rap industry. Most people would play it safe by sticking to what they know and try to "make it" in an industry filled with people from their demographic. However, Flex God Daps took the brave step of moving to America, where the competition was fierce, but he knew there were more opportunities.

He ended up meeting Coach K and Pee from Quality Control Records. They loved his perseverance and trusted him to direct the music videos of their most valuable artists. He directed music videos for Cardi B, Migos, and Lil Baby. His name grew further, which led to him directing music videos for Drake, Wizkid, Young Thug, and Davido. The irony is Daps ended up filming a music video for Stormzy, who is arguably the biggest rapper in the UK. If Daps stayed in the UK, he might never have got to the level to film Stormzy's videos, but he realised his core market wasn't in the same country as he was living in at the time. This enabled him to come full circle and have access to the top talent in the US and the UK.

Reggae/Dancehall artist Konshens is from Jamaica and had one of the most unconventional journeys in their music industry's history. In 2005, Konshens was in a duo called Sojah with his older brother, and they released a song called "Medz Pon Di Corner," which became popular in Japan. This led to Sojah having their first hit song and touring in a country not immediately associated with reggae/dancehall.

In 2006, Sojah released an album called "Sons of Jah," which was solely released in Japan. It may seem backwards to some people that they didn't release the album in Jamaica as well because it's the hub of reggae and dancehall. However, Sojah learned from the success of "Pon Di Corner" and decided to focus solely on an audience more likely to appreciate their product, even though it was outside of their demographic and norm.

Konshens had the burning desire to eventually flourish in his home country, so he decided to go solo in 2008. He used the experience and money gained in Japan to push his music in

Jamaica. He saw how tours helped grow his fan base rapidly, so he started organising small shows in Jamaica to help his music spread. Fast forward to 2012, Konshens released "Gyal a Bubble," which turned him into a superstar in Jamaica and brought him more international success in countries such as the UK and US.

At the time of writing, Konshens has over 320 million views on his YouTube channel. He has collaborated with Dutch EDM musician Eva Simons and American R&B singer Chris Brown. Konshens was willing to explore a market outside of his demographic, which not only brought him initial success but also provided him with the blueprint of how to succeed within his own demographic. Additionally, by collaborating with Eva Simons and Chris Brown, Konshens understands the power of having a fan base internationally, so he's now more open-minded than most artists due to his experience in Japan.

My friend Jerry was working as a trader in London for a Japanese bank whose headquarters are based in Tokyo. There was a vacancy in the Tokyo office, and his managers asked him if he could fill this role. Jerry was confused at first because he was wondering if they wanted him to pack up his whole life and move to another continent. His managers proposed he would initially work the same hours the Tokyo team worked (from London), and if he did well and he enjoyed it, there could be an opportunity to move to Tokyo.

Jerry decided to accept his managers' proposal and started work at 11 p.m. because this was 7 a.m. in Tokyo time. It took Jerry time to adjust to the working hours, the working culture, and the accent/language barrier. Over time, Jerry excelled in his new role and was offered a transfer date from his managers.

Jerry agreed to leave behind his friends, family, home, and ventures to move to a different continent because there were more opportunities for career growth in Tokyo. Jerry arrived in Tokyo in the middle of the pandemic, so he never had a good chance to settle in the country. Jerry didn't get to meet his new colleagues for months. It was ironic because he was working from home in Tokyo when he could have just stayed in London to do this.

Jerry bided his time until restrictions were eased and continued to work hard. Jerry decided to get a tutor to learn Japanese to amass himself in the culture and build deeper relationships when he returned to the office. When restrictions were finally eased, and Jerry began to work in the office, his new managers let him know they admired the work he put in from home in London and respected the fact he flourished working from a hotel in Tokyo.

Within a few months of being in the Tokyo office, Jerry received a major promotion that usually takes people in his position five to seven years to achieve, in comparison to the London office. His company also made him the face of multiple marketing campaigns as a success story, which gave him more notoriety. Jerry took the risk of moving to another country and stepped outside of his comfort zone. This led to a better pay package, major promotion, and notoriety in his industry.

In the London office, Jerry would have been that young guy who was born and raised in the city, who wanted the same promotion as everyone else in his position. Thus, he would have needed to do something extraordinary. In the Tokyo office, Jerry was that young guy who came from London, worked late nights there to keep up with Tokyo hours, left his friends and family to move to Tokyo in a pandemic, lived alone in a hotel in a new country, and hired a tutor to learn the language; so, in turn, he deserved the promotion because what he did was extraordinary.

It's very common to learn a new language when you move to another country; it's very common to stay by yourself in hotel rooms before settling in somewhere, and working nights is a norm in multiple job roles. However, in Jerry's case, these actions would have contributed to him standing out because they weren't the norm in his company. These actions also showcased someone who has desire, has belief in themself, is ambitious, and is willing to take risks. These are traits that get rewarded in most companies and contributed to Jerry's fast-tracked promotion.

If Jerry decides to move roles or organisations or start his own venture, he has a differentiator on his CV. Being able to succeed outside of your regular environment is extremely desirable for employers and investors. It indicates you are someone who can flourish in difficult environments and tackle different scenarios.

You should always explore other markets or countries to find where your product, services, or abilities will be best placed. Selecting your own country or demographic may turn out to be the lazy option and the one that leads to you not fulfilling your potential. However, moving to a different town, city, or country can be extremely risky if you don't plan accordingly.

Companies as big as Tesco have tried to tackle new markets and failed due to naivety and lack of planning. Tesco launched stores across the US in 2007 under the name Fresh & Easy. Tesco spent $1 billion on research and development, so they were confident they had done thorough planning. Tesco started by launching stores on the West Coast of America, where many people see driving to the supermarket as a weekly tradition. However, Tesco's naivety led them to think what works in the UK would work in the US.

In the UK, most of their popular stores were next to train stations, so they tried to adopt this strategy in the US. However, very few people use trains/subways in towns across the West Coast compared to the East Coast. Also, they made Fresh & Easy a mini-market rather than a superstore, so it was competing with the "mom & pop" local stores where the residents already had strong relationships with the shopkeepers.

Another assumption incorrectly made was that the customer service in the UK and US is similar. Fresh & Easy had self-checkout tills in store, which are used for convenience in Tesco's stores in the UK. However, Americans are known for valuing personal customer service to the point that giving tips is a strong part of their culture. Thus, they don't expect to pack their own shopping bags and found this to be a put-off with the Fresh & Easy store. There are many examples of stores that have self-checkout tills across the US currently, but this wasn't the case during the time Fresh & Easy were active.

In 2013, Tesco had to accept that Fresh & Easy was a failure, so they sold their stores, food production, and distribution centre to Yucaipa Companies. Tesco were brave enough to make a move to a foreign market, but they tried to use the same tactics that work in their home market abroad. This is a common pitfall of people and companies who take a step outside of their home market. Humans struggle to unlearn behaviour, and this becomes even more difficult when that behaviour has brought you success in the past. When you are going through your research and development stage, ensure you get a second set of eyes from someone who is from the new market or someone who has ventured outside their environment before. These are the types of people who will be able to easily spot naïve assumptions in your plans.

Moving abroad or your products to a new market comes with costs, so you're going to need enough capital to cover this. It's nice that Flex God Daps films music videos for top US artists and Konshens got to tour Japan, but they would have needed money to fund their stay. New countries come with new bills, new taxes, new insurances, etc. Before taking this step, you need to make sure you have saved up enough money to cover your lifestyle. If your success plan doesn't go in the way you wished, you can quickly run out of money trying to pursue your goal. It is unlikely you will have enough friends and family in the new country to fall back on to help with a place to stay, etc. Try to create a budget before you move, project potential costs, and see if the move is feasible. I would also recommend you have a "rainy day fund," which is money that should only be touched in emergencies. We will cover the importance of costs in chapter 10.

Go where the love is, and go where you're appreciated. In the previous chapter (Power of the Villain), I explained that it is harder to stand out when everyone is trying to be the hero. Similarly, it's hard to stand out when many people who share similar upbringings and experiences are all trying to do similar things in the hope of standing out. Therefore, you should seriously consider taking your products, services, or abilities to a new environment where you have more chance of being perceived as unique.

Thierry Henry is celebrated more in England than in France. Sometimes you're appreciated more outside your home.

CHAPTER 6

IN-HOUSE

A major lesson I learned from the *Black Girl Hair Documentary* was when you expect people to execute your vision in the manner you require, it can lead to issues.

I came up with the idea of the documentary and put together the cast but needed someone to film and edit it. I decided to reach out to my friend from college because I previously worked with him on a music video, so I knew what he could produce.

However, on this project, we quickly realised our working styles were totally opposite, which caused a few miscommunications. The documentary came out well, but looking back, I realised I set a standard in my head of how I thought things should be done, and he had a different way of doing things.

Fast forward to the second half of that year, I started Upper Echelon UK, which I describe as the "social hub for the elite." Before you call me a snob, please note "elite" refers to a mindset, not class or finances. Anyway, back to my point... Upper Echelon UK is a media, talent, and networking agency that aims to advance people who have talent and companies that have potential. This was all well and good, but who was going to do my filming and editing?... Oh, not this again.

I decided to keep things in-house by asking my friend Reemus to film and edit my first video because he was already a part of the Upper Echelon UK team, and we had worked well together previously on his Reemus Boxing brand. Reemus Boxing is a multimedia entertainment platform focused on boxing, which has amassed over twenty-three million views on YouTube and over seventy-five thousand subscribers.

In terms of Upper Echelon UK, Reemus filmed a video of me talking about my vision of the brand, and it received a lot of traction on social media and even led to the investor I mentioned in chapter 1 to reach out. However, Reemus was running his boxing platform, so he didn't have the time and capacity to keep up with the filming demands.

There were only two of us, and if he couldn't do it, how could I keep it in-house? You've probably guessed it… I realised I needed to learn how to film and edit. Reemus gave me a crash course lesson on filming and editing, and the rest of my learning came from YouTube.

I picked it up quite quickly, so my videos were coming out as I planned, which helped me move forward in the ways I envisioned. An early win came when I filmed and edited the behind-the-scenes of the *Day in the Life of Stephen (Stevie) Odubola*, who was the main character in the *Blue Story Movie*. It was surreal because I found myself on the red carpet of a film premiere with little to no experience. The day before the film premiere, I decided to shoot my shot by offering my services to Stevie, and he accepted. If you don't ask, you don't receive.

Upper Echelon UK has grown faster than expected because the lion share of our operations is in-house. Therefore, most things we do are within our control, which heightens the likelihood of execution. Outsourcing can be great sometimes, but when you keep things in-house, you learn the back-to-front process. Hence, a deeper understanding is one of the driving factors of high-execution levels. Filming and editing are excellent skills to have within your team if you run a business in this era because so much advertising is consumed on social media, which often requires video footage.

Another skill that can be a gamechanger for companies to have in-house is coding expertise. Being able to build applications, websites, and tailored software can improve efficiencies and take a company to the next level. Hence, acquiring this skill will mean you can save the money it would have taken to hire a coder. This money could be used in other parts of your business, for example, within the marketing department, so you can reach more people when advertising your products or services.

Learning how to code will provide you with a deeper understanding of the actual work that needs to be done if you eventually outsource or hire someone to join your company to take on the work. Coders are similar to mechanics because they are generally more knowledgeable about the action you are paying them to do. Therefore, some mechanics get away with charging people for things they didn't need and exaggerate issues, so they can charge higher prices.

If a coder tells you your project will cost £10,000 to build because of complexities you don't fully grasp, the only way you will be able to check if their price is "fair" is if you get prices from other coders. The issue with this is people can easily spot when someone isn't clued up on topics in their field, so if they realise you have a lack of knowledge, they can take advantage of you with the price and overestimate the time the job will take. Therefore, having the knowledge yourself will put you in a better position when you are trying to negotiate the length of time and price of the job with the vendor.

Michael Foote is the founder of Quote Goat, which is a comparison website for insurance, finance, and utilities. Michael had a desire to learn how to code because he wanted to start an online business but knew that he didn't have the funds to invest in a developer to do the coding. That's when he decided to set himself the challenge of creating a website within two months. He described the website as being "simple" and "effective."

Michael began to practice his coding skills more and more until it became natural. Michael wasn't a full-time developer; it was something he did on the side. He worked as a financial trader until the financial crash in 2007. The turmoil in the financial industry motivated Michael to focus his energy on using his coding skills to build his online comparison website, which he launched in 2008. Michael's comparison website was later rebranded as Quote Goat in 2014. Quote Goat is one of the leading comparison websites in the UK, and the foundation of its success was built on Michael learning how to code. This saved him a lot of money and enabled him to keep his operations in-house.

This chapter wasn't written to dissuade you from outsourcing; it was written to show you the advantages of keeping things in-house. Most companies that want to expand will eventually pursue outsourcing because it can help them grow. However, you shouldn't run before you can walk, so you should only spend money on outsourcing when you have used up your internal capabilities.

Outsourcing can provide you with more time to focus on the pivotal parts of your business, such as your customers. For example, if you have written the code for your website and outsourced the maintenance and bug fixing, you could use this extra time to create plans to attract and retain customers. Outsourcing also enhances your network because you will be working with external people who can provide new opportunities for your business. The developer you outsource the website maintenance to may have worked on similar websites before and knows a CEO of a car insurance provider who could offer cheap deals on your comparison website.

WhatsApp is a good example of a company that kept its operations in-house before outsourcing. Two former Yahoo employees, Brian Acton and Jan Koum, founded Whatsapp in 2009. They persuaded a few of their former Yahoo colleagues to get involved in their messaging service company as investors. WhatsApp noticed a gap in the market for a messaging service app on the Apple app store and later saw the same gap on the Blackberry app store, so it created two different versions to fit each store.

In 2012, the firm was operating with only thirty full-time employees and was based in California; however, they knew they needed assistance to deal with the demands of the growing users on the app. They decided to outsource to Russia, which offered developers at low costs with the required skills. The best-performing Russian developers were later relocated to the US office to bring their skills to the head office.

In 2014, WhatsApp was acquired by Facebook for $19 billion, which turned Brian and Jan into billionaires. Prior to this, they not only kept their operations in-house they also refused investment from countless venture capitalists. Hence, they still had large stakes within the company, so Jan earned $6.8 billion, and Brian earned $3.5 billion after taxes. These figures are astonishing considering they started the company a mere five years prior.

When you are selecting people to be a part of your company in the initial stages, don't just choose people because you get on with them. Try to select people who have specific skills or a network that can advance your business during the early stages. For example, a newly formed modelling agency should try to have a photographer, a videographer, an editor, and a fashion marketing specialist if possible. These people can help get the agency off the ground with pictures and videos showcasing their models on the right platforms. Consequently, their models would gain further exposure. This would also save money compared to hiring external vendors every time they need the content made and distributed.

Please don't fall into the trap of thinking these workers will be willing to work for free at your will. Many people are willing to work for free to build up a company without cutting into the budget. However, this won't last forever; these workers will begin to ask to be paid once they see money being made or when they feel like they are working too hard not to be paid. Also, there will be some people who buy into the vision but still want to be compensated straight away via a salary or ownership. It's always best to discuss the compensation package with each employee at the start, to minimise potential disagreements and unforeseen departures.

Ground-breaking psychologist Fredrick Herzberg put forward the Two-Factor Motivation Theory. "Hygiene" factors are linked to satisfaction: pay, relationship with colleagues, and working environment. "Motivation" factors centre around recognition, interest in work, and responsibility levels. The longer your employees are not paid, their satisfaction with the job will continue to descend (hygiene factor). However, you could try to combat the lack of pay by fostering great team morale and creating chemistry between your employees (hygiene factor).

In terms of motivation factors, you could try to combat the lack of pay by giving staff a higher job title and more responsibility than they would receive at a more established company. Your staff members would have already been sold on the vision because they were willing to work for free, so their interest in the job can't be questioned (motivation factor).

Keeping your operations in-house can save money and improve the back-to-front knowledge of the staff within your company. However, the staff need to feel satisfied and motivated to put the required work in that justifies the company not outsourcing.

Spend time sharpening your blade, so you know what is required to lead an army.

CHAPTER 7

FREE SAMPLES

Disclaimer… this whole chapter is controversial, but I know you're going to read on, so let me cut to the chase. Drug dealers are some of the most successful entrepreneurs who have walked this earth. They aren't mentioned in Business 101 books because of the poor morality of their business. What if we solely took the legal entrepreneurial gems from them and tried to use this to guide our own ventures?

"Freeway" Ricky Ross was estimated to have made around $600 million during the 1970s and 1980s by selling cocaine. Cocaine initially started as a "luxury drug" that only the rich and famous could afford. Still, people began to "stretch out" the product with different cooking methods to make it cheaper. This made cocaine more accessible for the middle and working classes, which caused US Presidents Richard Nixon and Ronald Reagan to push the "War on Drugs" initiative throughout the 1970s and 1980s.

Ricky Ross grew up poor, then had to endure the government's fight against the field he was working in, so it begs the question: how was he so successful? Ricky knew cocaine was perceived as an expensive drug, so he had to change how the drug was viewed by the middle and working classes. Ricky came across a cooking formula that could multiply cocaine whilst arguably making the drug more effective. This was a win-win for him because his product became more enhanced, and the amounts he could make from the same package also increased. This new product was later called "crack," which I'm sure you have heard of.

Ricky now had a cheaper product but still had to make it competitive in comparison to the other drugs on the black market, such as cannabis and heroin. This was when he decided to give out free samples to his target market because he was confident in the quality and price point of his product. Ricky was a big believer in "If your work is good, it will sell," so he didn't view free samples as a waste of potential revenue. He knew his product would sell once people had a taste of it. Crack was much cheaper and more addictive than the other drugs at the time, so it was no surprise Ricky went on to be a multimillionaire and a big contributor to the crack epidemic in the 1980s.

This is the part where I don't make criminals sound like heroes. Ricky eventually was arrested and served prison time due to his drug enterprise. Ironically, he was set up by his supplier, who became a police informant after being caught himself. Please do not think I am encouraging you to commit crimes; just take the legal gems out of Ricky's Blueprint, e.g., the free samples tactic.

The black market and free samples go hand-in-hand because the supplier cannot advertise their product or show reviews as freely as legal products. Therefore, the easiest way to prove the validity of the product is by letting people try it for free. However, free samples can be an extremely effective way to drive up demand in the regular legal market. It is common for people to tell their friends and family about a product they received for free, especially if they liked it. Word of mouth is a powerful marketing tool, so giving out free samples is a great way to encourage people to spread the word about your product.

In 2009, I went with my family to watch Usain Bolt run at the London Aviva Grand Prix at Crystal Palace National Sports Centre. We're Jamaican, so it was a great day seeing Bolt live for the first time, especially after the gold medal successes he had at the Beijing Olympics the year before. Unsurprisingly, Bolt won all his races at Crystal Palace and put us all in a good mood as we left the stadium. As soon as we exited, we were approached by people who were giving out free samples of a shower gel called Original Source: Mint and Tea Tree.

My brother Omar and I took one each and promised the guy who gave us the sample that we'd try it the next morning. I remember Omar waking me up by telling me this new shower gel felt weird, and he was not sure how to describe the feeling and told me to let him know once I used it. After I used it, I remember describing it as being "tingly and strange," and I said I wouldn't use it again. Fast forward one week later, and I see two full-size bottles of this shower gel in our bathroom cabinet. Omar clearly enjoyed that strange feeling.

If you think I am exaggerating the feeling, there was an article in the *Metro* (2017) that said, "Using Original Source's mint and tea tree shower gel on your vulva or near your bits is not wise, it hurts." Okay... this article was for women, and I don't have a vulva, but you get the picture here. Nonetheless, Omar was sold on the shower gel and became a repeat customer because Original Source was stocked up in our bathroom cabinet until Omar eventually moved out.

I'm sure Omar wasn't the only person who appreciated the free sample in Crystal Palace, so I know he wouldn't have been the only one who became a repeat customer. Original Source showcased how effective giving out free samples can be, especially at the right location. Crystal Palace National Sports Centre has a capacity of over 15,000, so you can take a guess on how many of those people became future customers or recommended the product to friends and family.

Free samples are a powerful tool because you're introducing new people to your product or service who can turn into future customers. This strategy also leads to more reviews and feedback, so it can build trust around your product or services quicker than if you waited for that same amount of people to make purchases. Thus, other people will feel more at ease purchasing your product or service after reading the reviews online or hearing about it via word of mouth.

Reciprocity is the notion that it is the social norm for people to respond with a positive action when they receive a positive action. Sociologist Phillip Kunz (1974) mailed Christmas cards to roughly 600 strangers and nearly received over 200 replies. This shows that over one-third of people were willing to reciprocate a nice gesture from a stranger. In terms of free sampling, the person who received the free product or service may decide to leave you a nice review online, persuade friends and family to purchase, or even apply to become an employee of the company!

If I asked you right now, "WHERE'S THE MONEY!?" you can point towards the revenue that will be made from all the new customers that come from the free samples; however, free samples come at a cost (chapter 10)! You need to make sure you budget the amount that you are willing to spend on free samples and forecast the results you realistically expect to achieve. There's no point spending most of your company's funds on luring in new customers if you don't have enough cash flow to cover the company's operating costs (rent, travel, insurance, etc.)

Costs are not the only downside to giving out free samples. Perception is extremely important to companies because a strong brand image can lead to sales. Some people may have a bad experience with the free sample because they may feel as though the product given was too small, and that can lead to them thinking the company isn't generous. Additionally, if the product was given to them outside a train station when they were in a rush to get to work, they may blame your company for slowing them down and making them late for work. Thus, the location and approach of the staff can lead to negative perceptions as well.

Some people are greedy, so they may continuously take advantage of your free sample, which blocks other customers from having the chance to try your product. The free sample strategy is implemented to lead to sales, but this strategy won't be effective if people continuously enjoy your product without spending. Additionally, there will be other people who will take your free sample and never use it. Some people feel awkward saying no, so they will throw your product in the closest bin out of the vision of the person who just handed them your product.

There is no doubt that free samples can lead to money being wasted; however, *Supermarket News* (2005) reported free samples can increase sales by up to 2,000%. It is important to select the right staff, location, and profile of potential customers before giving out free samples. Staff are arguably the most important factor because they set the first impression the customer receives from the company. Thus, the level of pressure the staff applies can be make or break in terms of if the customer will buy the product in the future. Heilman et al. (2011) found "samplers with a heightened awareness of the presence of others at the sampling station may feel a level of social 'pressure' to make a post-sample purchase." Thus, the potential customer's perception of the way the staff conducts themselves can be a major factor in terms of the sale of the product.

If you want to try out the free samples approach, you should begin with establishing your target audience. Once you have done this, try to dig into their interests and find out where a good amount of your target audience can be found and the optimal date and time. Then you should carefully select the staff to do the outreach. These can be people you know personally, people you find via a job advertisement or people provided by an agency.

Selecting people you know personally can be a strong choice because they may be more likely to project the passion you have for your company because they want to see you succeed. However, they may not have experience doing outreach work, so their persuasive skills may be lacking. Hiring staff from a job advertisement can work because the staff would have read the job description and would have to pass your interview questions, so they will have the knowledge to answer the questions of potential customers. However, they may only be doing the job for the money, so they may not showcase the passion required to sell the brand to the potential customer. Using agency staff can work well because they are likely to have done outreach work previously, so they will probably have good persuasive skills. However, they may not have the knowledge required to go into enough details about your product to satisfy the potential customer.

There are pros and cons of the different approaches for selecting staff, so there isn't one perfect approach. I would advise you to select people from a mixture of the different approaches, then monitor their performance, so you know how to get the right balance in the future. The product isn't the only thing that needs to be tested by the potential customer; the type of staff member also needs to be tested to see what strategy works best. Alternatively, if you are in a position where you already employ staff, you can ask them to do the outreach because they should already have the passion and knowledge of the brand, and you can train them to improve their outreach skills.

Another thing to consider is the demographic of your target customer. If your target customers are teenage girls, there is no point having men who are 60+ years old doing the outreach. The company may have been started by people who are not in the demographic of the target customers, but you need to select staff who will appeal and relate to the customers to do the outreach.

Free samples can be a game-changer if efficient planning has been put in place because it can lead to an influx of purchases. Providing your target customer with the opportunity to test out your product or service is usually received as an act of kindness, so it can lead to favourable results via reciprocity. The free samples strategy is a great way to attract customers, but the next hurdle is your ability to retain them. Turning these new customers into repeat customers showcases the effectiveness of your plan and displays high levels of execution.

Everyone likes to try before they buy.

CHAPTER 8

GIVING BACK

Many people believe you must be ruthless to be successful in business. "It's a dog-eat-dog world" and "Nice guys finish last" are two famous phrases that are closely related to this ideology. This stems from an individualistic culture that pits people against each other rather than promoting collaboration and selflessness. Culture can be defined as "the way things are done around here." Therefore, if you change the way things are done, you can change the culture.

In 1992, Fairtrade certified products became available to buy across the UK. Fairtrade products are those that use labelling to declare to the customer that the money spent on the product will go towards helping the producers get a fairer deal from the exporter. Many of these producers came from developing countries and were previously getting exploited with low prices being forced upon them. Goods such as sugar, cocoa, fruit, flowers, and coffee are examples of Fairtrade products.

Fairtrade products began to become a trendy commodity because the consumers liked that they were helping people every time they purchased these products. This encouraged more companies to get into this business because it was like having a blue tick on social media; the label made you more popular. Fairtrade products clearly show companies can take the "nice guy approach" and still be successful.

Fast forward to present times, and you can see countless examples of companies giving back. House of CB is a luxury womenswear brand founded by Conna Walker, who made it onto *Forbes*' 30 under 30's list in 2019. One contributing factor to Conna's success is her selflessness because she often gives back to upcoming female entrepreneurs. She set up a competition where she had three cash prizes of £10k, £5k, and £2k for three winners. The competition normally leads to House of CB trending on social media, positive headlines in the press, and more purchases from first-time buyers. The £17k spent on the winners will be recouped from the additional sales, and the perception of the company also improves.

You can be crude and argue that Conna Walker only does this competition to raise the profile and profits of House of CB. Even if this was the case, she is also improving the trajectory of the careers of three female entrepreneurs, which is a great thing to do for other people. This is no different than a company that sells coffee deciding to sell Fairtrade products because they know it will perform better than non-Fairtrade products. Some may say it is poor ethics to benefit from a good cause and to make money from it. However, other people will say the main thing is the producers are now being given a fairer deal, which wasn't happening before, so this is ethically okay. It's nice to be nice to people; not every business culture needs to be dog-eat-dog.

<u>I'll give you three scenarios that relate to giving back.</u>

1. Someone gives £10 to a homeless person, then posts a selfie with the homeless person without consent

2. Someone drops £1 in the homeless person's cup and walks off without saying "Hi."

3. Someone has a two-minute conversation with a homeless person, asking about their life, and treated them with respect. However, refused to give them money.

Scenario 1

Pro: £10 is a generous amount, considering most people just leave coins.

Con: It seems like the giver is just doing it to look good on social media without considering the feelings of the homeless person.

Scenario 2

Pro: £1 is a nice gesture to give to someone in need.

Con: The giver could have at least acknowledged the homeless person as a mark of respect.

Scenario 3

Pro: Treating the homeless person with respect and dignity is admirable because this can help the homeless person receive emotional support that they may have been craving.

Con: They could have given money as well because even a small amount would contribute towards food or a beverage for someone in need.

There will always be people who will have something negative to say, even when you're making a nice gesture, so just go with your gut and stick with it. Please remember, "Every time someone helps you, they are also helping themselves," whether that's financial via additional sales or emotionally via feeling good about themselves. You shouldn't feel guilty when doing the same because nearly every human interaction is an exchange.

If you are wondering how you can come up with an idea for a generous initiative, the first place to start is with the skills you already have. Airbnb is a revolutionary company that helped change the market of overnight stays via their home-sharing online marketplace. Traditionally, people used to predominately use hotels when they needed to find somewhere to stay overnight. However, Airbnb made it a norm to pay to use someone else's vacant home.

Airbnb has the skill of connecting vendors of vacant homes with people who need somewhere to stay, so they used this skill to start their OpenHomes initiative. OpenHomes provides a temporary place for people to stay who have been affected by illness, conflict, and natural disasters in their home countries. The OpenHomes concept was formulated in 2012 and was inspired by a host who made her home available to people affected by Hurricane Sandy.

Another way you can put together a nice initiative is by assessing the current climate and aiding the resolution of a current societal issue. Airbnb noticed that the frontline workers during the coronavirus pandemic were risking their family's lives and their own by potentially being exposed to COVID-19 daily. Airbnb decided to add frontline workers to their OpenHomes initiative and provided discounted and free homes to stay in near the frontline workers' places of work.

One of the most fun and traditional ways to give back is via a fundraising event. JP Morgan began its annual Corporate Challenge in 1977. The JP Morgan Corporate Challenge is a 3.5-mile run, and it is open to corporate workers from a range of different companies who team up and compete in the race. This event not only promotes camaraderie, teamwork, and fun; it also raises money for charity every year. By being the host, JP Morgan gains brand exposure to potential new employees. A high-performing employee from a rival company may see JP Morgan in a more favourable light after raising money and running in this event. As mentioned previously, perception is vital in terms of the success of a company, so the Corporate Challenge can provide JP Morgan with good press, new clients, and new employees.

You need to be careful when giving back because some people become too absorbed with the benefits they will receive rather than being focused on the help they are providing. Arguably, the most fatal example of this came in Bangladesh when a goodwill initiative increased the chances of death for millions of people.

In the 1970s, thousands of people were dying from drinking dirty water in Bangladesh, so UNICEF and the Department of Public Health Engineering worked together to install tube-wells with "safe" and "clean" water. However, the water was only tested for purity, and they didn't test it for arsenic, which is poisonous. This led to millions of people drinking contaminated water and the death of thousands. The survivors suffered as well because arsenic can lead to skin, lung, and bladder cancer. Many people also developed skin lesions, such as pigmentation changes and keratosis. The World Health Organisation described it as "the largest mass poisoning of a population in history."

I would firstly like to say "Rest in peace" to all the people who lost their lives and condolences to those who suffered or are suffering health issues due to an unfortunate misjudgement. UNICEF is one of the most famous organisations for giving back and providing relief for major issues, so if they can get decisions fatally wrong, so can you. People who give back need to put all their energy into providing the solutions for the person or people in need rather than planning what the success of the initiative can do for them personally. I believe if you do good, then good things will happen to you, so you should stay tunnel-visioned with the task at hand rather than focusing on the potential benefits that could come from it.

When you are in the planning process, run it by people who have managed similar campaigns or people who have experience in the area you are venturing into. UNICEF tried to collaborate with the Department of Public Health Engineering because they felt they would cover the expertise required for this initiative. However, they should have had multiple independent surveyors do checks on the tube-wells because this probably would have led to arsenic being detected. Try to cover as many blind spots as possible before launching your initiative because something that started off as a goodwill gesture can ruin your company image forever.

You need to be careful about the cause you are supporting because this can dissuade people from purchasing goods or services from your company. The National Rifle Association of America (NRA) is one of the most powerful advocacy groups in the US. The NRA acts as a pressure group to the government to uphold gun rights, so many individuals and companies donate money to them. If customers who are anti-gun rights find out a CEO or company donates large sums of money towards the NRA, this could put them off spending money with that company.

Tax is a double-edged sword when it comes to giving back. When a limited company donates money, it can receive tax reliefs. Donations can be accounted for as a business expense, so it reduces the profits, which in turn lowers the corporation tax to be paid. Thus, giving money to a good cause can help other people and provide tax benefits for the company. However, this can negatively affect your company's public perception. If media publications begin to publish stories about your company using charity donations to lower taxes and hide genuine expenses, this can make your company seem disingenuous and fraudulent. Therefore, if you are giving back, please ensure you are as transparent as possible, so the media struggle to paint a negative picture of your positive actions.

Your greatness is not what you have; it's what you give.

CHAPTER 9

REPETITION AND CONSISTENCY

You're probably thinking, "Did I really spend my money on a book that has a whole chapter on reputation and consistency!?" Yes... you sadly did. However, if you read on, you'll realise the chapter is not dull like you imagined.

I'm sure you have heard phrases such as "Try, try and try again" and "10,000 hours will turn you into an expert." Both phrases centre around "repetition" and "consistency." When you repeat an action over and over again, you become more knowledgeable and skilful. However, the other benefit most people fail to realise is repetition and consistency make other people take notice of you.

You will begin to change the way other people perceive you. People will start to see you as a hard worker and will grow comfortable in accepting you being attached to the action you have been executing. An example of this can be seen with the singer Conor Maynard. He made a name for himself by being relentless with the number of song covers he performed on his YouTube Channel. The comments on his videos consisted of things like "Crazy work rate" and "You deserve to make it, buddy."

Maintaining consistency and executing repetition allowed Conor to improve his singing ability and improve the way the public perceived him. Most people like a "trier" and the underdog story. It shows your hunger when you show them consistency. This hunger also shows them that you are not currently at the place you want to be, so they will feel the responsibility of helping you get there. This could be by simply spreading the word or spending money on what you have to offer. Conor eventually went on to have the number-one album in the UK (Contrast) in 2012. Conor built up a powerful fan base who felt like they were on the journey with him and still were willing to do their bit to take a "trier" to the next level.

A more recent example of repetition and consistency can be seen with Uwe Baltner, who also sings covers of songs… but badly. Uwe decided to sing a new song every day in his car and put it on his Instagram. His singing wasn't great, and his car was mediocre at best. People began to admire his consistency, so decided to recommend him new songs. This is an example of how repetition and consistency can lead to public interaction because they feel responsible for helping a "trier" on their journey. His fans thought it would be funny if Uwe covered a rap song, so he decided to give it ago. Uwe knew he would be laughed at by his friends and the public, but he believed in the process of repetition and consistency.

The rap songs ended up being an express train to success for Uwe. He realised people found it hilarious that a middle-aged white man was doing covers of rap songs. There is real marketing power in using your stereotype to your advantage (chapter 4).

"WHERE'S THE MONEY!?" If this wasn't in your head already, you might need to go back and read chapter 1. Uwe began to charge musicians a fee to cover their songs and post them on his platform. He currently has over 1.5 million followers, so many artists see his page as a perfect platform to promote their music. They know his followers are willing to give a chance to new music, so it makes sense for them to pay Uwe for advertisement.

Uwe managed to battle through being laughed at by using repetition and consistency as his weapons. Eventually, he was able to generate income from something that started off as a bit of fun because he was smart enough to monetise his service.

Repetition and consistency are the most powerful tools in terms of creating an expert. You can be talented at something, but unless you gain experience doing it repeatedly, it will be unlikely that you get to a level people consider as "expert." Tennis player Rafael Nadal is naturally right-handed, but he is world-renowned for playing with his left hand. Nadal worked tirelessly on his left hand to the point that it became his dominant hand whilst playing tennis.

Nadal has an advantage in most tennis matches he plays because he is used to facing opponents who play with their right hand, but most of his opponents are not used to playing against people who play with their left. One of Nadal's fiercest competitors, Roger Federer, asked him in an interview why he plays with his left hand instead of his right because it has been a problem for him over the years. Nadal confirmed he is naturally right-handed but alternated between right and left when he was young, then settled on his left.

Nadal used repetition and consistency to such a high level throughout his youth that he was able to play elite-level tennis with his "so-called" weaker hand. Nadal is one of the most decorated tennis players of all time due to winning over ninety tennis titles throughout his career (singles and doubles).

You should apply Nadal's approach and use repetition and consistency in your own life. For example, a pâtissier (pastry/dessert chef) could research desserts that most people find difficult to make and focus their time on these. If the pâtissier uses repetition and consistency to devote themselves to making these desserts, they could fast track themselves in terms of being known as an elite chef. Instead of spending time learning how to make the most common desserts, the pâtissier can place themselves up-market and be renowned for serving desserts that are rare. Therefore, they will be able to charge higher prices for their desserts and gain more notoriety in their industry by focusing on something that will give them an advantage via repetition and consistency.

Let's not be naïve, though; you can't beat a dead horse. Repetition and consistency are powerful tools, but if you don't have a natural talent or ability to do something at a high level, you need to know the difference between quitting and moving on. Martha Stewart was a full-time model, but her career began to go on a downward trajectory after she became a mother in her mid-twenties. She knew she had to put in extra work to get her body to the point it was prior to pregnancy.

Martha wanted to prove to herself and others she could still be a successful model post-pregnancy. Martha spent time working on her fitness, health, and body, along with continuously applying for multiple modelling jobs. However, opportunities became few and far between, and repetition and consistency were not effective in terms of Martha's modelling ambitions.

Martha had two options: either "quit" or keep pursuing her modelling dreams. Martha decided to use the time and effort she was putting into modelling to pursue a career as a Wall Street stockbroker. Martha worked as a stockbroker for half a decade but realised she wasn't happy because she felt like she wasn't pursuing her actual passion. Her mother taught her how to cook, and it was something she did a lot in her spare time but never pursued professionally.

Martha's ex-husband, Andrew Stewart, was the president of a successful publishing company called Harry N. Abrams, Inc. and released the English language version of *The Secret*

Book of Gnomes. This book became a major success and was on *The New York Times* Best Seller list. Andrew decided to ask Martha to cater the book's release party, and this was where she met the head of Crown Publishing Group, Alan Mirken.

Alan was enthralled by Martha's aura and cooking skills, so he decided to offer her a book deal. Martha's first book was *Entertaining*, and the success of this led to many more book releases, her own magazine, and television show. Martha is an excellent example of someone who knew when the right time to "quit" was. She realised modelling wasn't working, so she moved on to stockbroking. Then she realised she wasn't happy doing stock broking, so she decided to pursue her passion, cooking.

Martha's journey should be familiar to many people because when we're young, we feel as though the sky is the limit, so we pursue our dreams, in her case, modelling. Then when we get a harsh taste of reality, we realise the "real world" provides challenges that can block our dreams. At this point, many people take a safer, more proven career choice and suppress their interests for money. This can be seen when Martha took a job as a stockbroker. This stage is a differentiator because many people stay in that "safe and proven" job until they retire and go through stages, saying things like "I wish I did X when I was younger." This approach leads to stability, but it can make people feel as though they wasted their potential, which is a prominent cause of a mid-life crisis.

Martha decided to not accept "safe and proven" and pursued another passion, cooking. There was no guarantee of success, but Martha knew cooking made her happy, and the financial crash on Wall Street made her notice that her stockbroking job wasn't as stable as she thought. That is another element we should consider because people often look at 9-5 jobs as stable, but we are all aware of sackings, redundancies, and companies that collapsed.

There is no such thing as a stable job, so you should at least try your hand at your passion by using the repetition and consistency tools to move forward on your journey. Try to set yourself a time limit in terms of how long you plan to pursue your goal before looking into alternatives. Martha's journey should show you that she gave herself time to succeed at her first passion, modelling, and even though it didn't go the way she wanted, she was able to pursue another passion in the future, and cooking became her key to success.

Repetition and consistency are very effective tools, but you should use your gut to know if you should move on from what you were originally trying to achieve. Unfortunately, we cannot be great at everything, so spending too long trying to attain a skill you are failing to grasp can lead to missing out on your undiscovered talents.

"The longer you entertain what is not for you, the longer you postpone what is."

Only you will know when the right time to move on is, so all I can say is don't stop at the first hurdle and keep going until you can't convince yourself of realistic reasons to continue. You should also consult trusted friends and family to provide constructive views to assist with your decision.

Repetition and consistency may sound bland and obvious, but perfecting simple things is the foundation of greatness.

CHAPTER 10

DON'T FORGET COSTS!

One of my friends, Alex, told me about a business idea he felt passionately about, and you can probably guess that I asked him: "WHERE'S THE MONEY!?" He actually gave me a great response, and I was only able to pick out a couple holes in his plan. I felt like "WHERE'S THE MONEY!?" had finally been defeated. The competitive nature inside me shot out, and I asked, "What about costs!?" As he ran me through his costs, I quickly realised that even though he had a great idea and plan to make revenue, his costs were way too high.

My friends will tell you, "Ish loves to play devil's advocate," and even though I know it's annoying, it's all about maximising the chances of execution. It's better to pick holes in a plan in private rather than your finished product having holes in public. If you were there to hear the first half of our conversations and compare it to the second half, you'd truly see the definition of "There's a thin line between love and hate."

I began to suggest ways Alex could reduce costs, such as bulk buying, spending more time looking for a cheaper supplier, reducing shipping costs, etc. The week after, Alex told me how he couldn't get "WHERE'S THE MONEY!?" out of his head, which made him think of further ways to increase revenue, which would reduce the impact his costs have on his profits. Alex now had a good idea, multiple ways to make revenue, and a strategy to reduce his costs.

It's human nature to see the prize rather than what goes into making or achieving that prize. It's not only business owners who face this problem. Mike Tyson was worth around $300 million at the peak of his net worth but filed for bankruptcy in 2003. It's understandable if you're scratching your head right now. You're probably thinking that if you had all that money, there is no way you could become bankrupt. Well, let's dive deeper into the importance of costs.

In simple terms, Mike Tyson was overspending and gaining debt to live a lifestyle he desired. He wasn't strategically thinking about his costs in comparison to the amount he earned because keeping up his desired lifestyle was more important to him. This behaviour isn't any different than people who live cheque to cheque and use a credit card or overdraft to maintain their lifestyle. If someone earns £30,000 in a year and lives in a city apartment that costs £2,000 a month to rent, that is already £24,000 gone (in a year) without considering taxes. Therefore, people will use a credit card to keep up with other payments, such as transport, food, fashion, and utility bills.

"It's not about what you make; it's about what you spend." When Mike Tyson went bankrupt, he owed $23 million in debt. You could argue that a guy on a £20,000 annual salary with no debt and who lives free of charge at his parents' house would be more financially stable than Mike would have been in 2003. Ironically, the guy on £20,000 a year would arguably be more financially stable than the guy who earns £30,000 with £2,000 monthly rent and credit card debts. Cost is the least glamourous word in the "revenue – cost = profit" formula because it relates to losing rather than gaining. However, there is a lot to gain if you can keep your costs low as a business or an individual.

Richard Wagoner was the CEO of General Motors (GM) between 2000-2009. In 2003, he was profusely questioned by the media on his cost strategy. He explained that fixed costs are high in the automobile industry, so GM lowered the prices of their vehicles rather than reducing volume. He felt as though this strategy enabled GM to still make money in a high-cost market. Richard ended up losing GM over $82 billion during his tenure as CEO of the company. He was eventually pressured into resigning by the Obama administration because the U.S. government had to intervene to aid survival.

Richard's strategy of lowering the price in the hope of driving up sales to cover high costs failed completely. He should have focused on lowering costs before attempting to drive up the revenue. Richard could have reduced the volume of cars that were being made at the time. The customers were already used to paying the current price, so if there were fewer cars in the market, that could have made the demand higher than the supply.

Alternatively, Richard could have tried to increase the prices of their cars to coincide with the scarcity of the cars due to lower volumes. This could have had a trickle-down effect on used cars because they would also hold value longer. After all, the new models would then be rarer and more expensive. This strategy could have enhanced the public's perception of General Motors because their cars would be closely aligned to premium rather than standard products.

However, in 2009, many people were suffering economically due to the global recession on the back of the financial crisis. Raising the prices of cars may not have been sensible at that time because consumers had less money to spend, so there was no need to continue producing cars at that current rate. Therefore, Richard should have focused on changing the volume rather than the price because lowering the volume lowers the costs, so profits could still be improved.

If Richard had kept the prices the same, the demand could still have increased because he could have used data analytics to pinpoint the demand level to ensure that GM's supply was lower. GM could have enhanced the perception of their brand if their cars were perceived as being rarer than previously, making them more desirable.

In 2007, gaming company Zynga was launched, and by 2009, they became one of Facebook's most successful app developers due to their game *Farmville*. Zynga began to grow rapidly because they were flourishing on the biggest social media platform at the time. In 2012, Zynga reported over $300 million in revenue and 300 million active monthly users of their games. That same year, Zynga noticed that many of their customers moved away from desktops and were using Facebook via their mobile phones. Instead of spending time developing quality games that would fit the smaller screen, Zynga decided to take a costly shortcut.

Zynga spent $180 million acquiring OMGPOP, who created the popular *Draw Something* game, which was built as a mobile phone app. Unfortunately, Zynga made this purchase at the summit of the game's popularity and ended up writing off nearly $95 million due to the failure of OMGPOP. Zynga also spent $228 million on their headquarters, which was based in San Francisco.

In 2013, Zynga lost more than half of their user base from the year before and had to let go of 520 employees. They also closed their Los Angeles, Dallas, and New York City offices. One year later, things remained bleak because they had to let go of an additional 314 employees.

Zynga is an example of a company that simply didn't consider costs. They were having unprecedented amounts of success for an online gaming company and got caught up in the dream of exponential growth rather than formulating a realistic plan to keep moving forward. When Zynga faced their first major problem, they decided to throw money at it rather than strategically formulating a plan to adjust to the issue. When online gaming began to move from desktops to mobile phones, they should have been working on ways to adjust their existing games, be compatible with mobile phones, and keep up with the demand in the new market. While they were learning the mobile phone market with their existing games, they could have been developing new games simultaneously. This would have provided something fresh for their customers.

Converting their existing games and developing new games to be mobile phone friendly would have come at a cost and would have taken longer than acquiring OMGPOP. However, Zynga would have had the opportunity to carefully tailor games to their customers and not have to spend $180 million on a "quick fix." The costs would have been spread over time as well because they would be finding out new pieces of helpful information throughout their research and development stage, which would indicate how to allocate their budget over time. The dream of growth can be exciting when it seems in touching distance, so you need to consider costs before letting your excitement lead to naive decisions.

People often ignore costs when they get wrapped up in competition with other people. They may feel as though their ego and pride are under threat, so they want to "win at all costs"; no pun intended. A clear example of this was seen in the 1990s and early 2000s when the World Wrestling Federation (WWF) and World Championship Wrestling (WCW) competed for TV ratings on Monday evenings. The rivalry was coined *The Monday Night Wars*, and it has also been described as the "golden era of wrestling." WWF (currently called WWE) was owned by Vince McMahon, and WCW was owned by Ted Turner. Vince McMahon and Ted Turner were bitter rivals. They used to goad each other on their respectful shows, making their rivalry public.

Ted Turner saw the success of WWF and wanted to compete, so he began to poach their most prominent stars, such as Hulk Hogan and Randy "Macho Man" Savage. WCW gave out lucrative long-term contracts to many wrestlers to persuade them to leave WWF for WCW. Ted Turner also paid for the services of musicians to try to stand out from WWF in the hope that their popularity would raise WCW's ratings. WCW signed rapper Master P for $293,000 to wrestle and reportedly paid rock band KISS $500,000 to do a very short live performance. Basketball player Dennis Rodman also made headlines for getting paid $1.6 million for wrestling in only three matches. Unsurprisingly, in the year 2000, WCW lost $60 million and were struggling with their show's ratings.

Ted Turner let his rivalry with Vince McMahon lead him to overspend because he wanted to win at all costs. A large portion of WCW's financial difficulties came from the lucrative long-term contracts they gave to former WWF wrestlers because they weren't earning enough to cover these costs. When WCW was giving out these contracts, they were only thinking about the short-term win of making WWF look bad, and themselves look superior. WCW totally ignored costs and the long-term health of the company.

There was another storm brewing in the background because Ted Turner's company (Turner Broadcasting System, Inc.) merged with Time Warner. Time Warner later merged with AOL to create AOL Time Warner. The bosses at Time Warner initially put pressure on Ted Turner to reduce the costs of WCW. Still, he couldn't do this because of the lucrative long-term contracts he agreed with multiple different people. After the AOL merger, the bosses reviewed WCW's finances. They were mortified by the losses WCW were making due to its high costs. Ironically, AOL Time Warner decided to sell WCW to Vince McMahon for only $2.5 million in 2001. Vince McMahon added salt in Ted Turner's wounds when he bragged about the situation on live TV and said things like "I own my own competition" and "Time Warner is practically begging me to buy WCW." To make matters worse, he even named Ted Turner personally when he said, "I'll sign it when Ted Turner himself walks down the aisle at Wrestlemania and delivers the contract in front of me."

Ouch! I'm sure Ted Turner would have reflected on all the money he spent at WCW over the years and his lack of care towards costs. These mishaps are similar to the Zynga example because Ted Turner tried to throw money when trying to grow (lucrative contracts) and at his problems (ratings dropping). Ted should have spent time developing his own wrestlers, storylines, and entertainment. This would have enabled WCW to focus on its long-term existence rather than short-term wins. Hulk Hogan was the biggest star WWF had, so it made sense to take him for the publicity and the fans, and he delivered. However, this is where Ted should have stopped. Once Hulk Hogan helped to increase the viewership of WCW, they should have focused on internal development rather than paying out large sums to other WWF stars and celebrities.

As you know, the title of this book is "WHERE'S THE MONEY!?" because I want people to ask themselves this question in business scenarios they face. Sometimes we let our passions, dreams, or naivety get in the way of capitalising economically on things we put our energy into. The goal is to make money to provide yourself with access to things that can provide security and joy to yourself and others. However, you cannot achieve this if your costs are too high. Some people earn £70,000 a year but stay in expensive apartments in the city, go out to bars and restaurants multiple times a week, and regularly buy the latest clothes. There are other people on £30,000 a year who live in modest apartments, go out to bars and restaurants once a week, and only buy clothes when they are going out to events.

There is no right or wrong approach, but there are many people who are on £30,000 a year who live within their means and have more money in their current and savings account than people on £70,000 a year. How much you spend is more important than how much you earn, which is why someone as rich as Mike Tyson was bankrupt at one point. You should enjoy your life and create memories, but always keep it in the back of your mind that you cannot have an abundance if you spend abundantly.

Costs are equally as important for individuals and companies because spending more than what has been earned or not having enough liquid funds to pay your outflows will lead to stress, regardless of if it's a personal or business account. Budgeting is extremely important and needs to be taken seriously to avoid ending up in bad situations like the ones mentioned in this chapter.

What's the point of having a swimming pool if you can't afford to maintain it?

CLOSING STATEMENT

Now I have officially read three books (including my own)!

All jokes aside, I am proud to have finished my first book and glad you have taken the time out to read it. I decided to try something new during the coronavirus pandemic, and I can now add "author" to my CV. "Try" always makes me giggle in my head because when I was little, my mum used to always say, "Don't cry, try." Maybe that's where I developed the confidence to try new things.

If you enjoyed this book, please use me as an example of someone who was willing to try something totally out of their comfort zone. I hope it inspires you to reach a point of being comfortable, being uncomfortable. Once you go through stages such as being laughed at, you will develop thick skin and get used to battling awkward situations. I would love for you to contact me and share a story of how you tried something new and what you achieved from taking that step.

One of my favourite quotes comes from Thomas Edison: "Vision without execution is hallucination." If you have an idea you don't implement, it will become a dream rather than reality. The goal should always be to bring your ideas to life, so you can unleash your true potential.

Before I let you go, I want to leave you with one piece of advice:

The best time to start was yesterday.

www.ingramcontent.com/pod-product-compliance
Ingram Content Group UK Ltd.
Pitfield, Milton Keynes, MK11 3LW, UK
UKHW020135250726
13967UKWH00002B/678